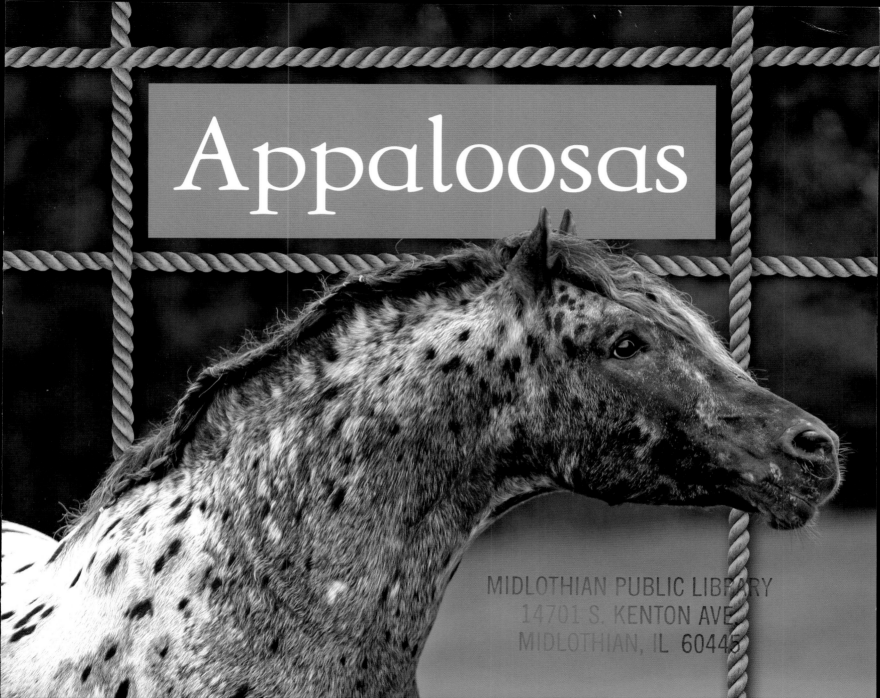

Appaloosas

The Child's World®

Published by The Child's World®
1980 Lookout Drive • Mankato, MN 56003-1705
800-599-READ • www.childsworld.com

Acknowledgments
The Child's World®: Mary Berendes, Publishing Director
The Design Lab: Design
Jody Jensen Shaffer: Editing
Red Line Editorial: Photo Research

Photo credits
bojangles /Shutterstock.com: 20; Ellustrations.iStock.com: 6; Eric
Isselee/Shutterstock.com: 22-23; Joe Belanger/Shutterstock.com:
rope; Lenkadan/Shutterstock.com: 11, 16; Kersti Nebelsiek/
Wikimedia Commons, 12; Margo Harrison/Shutterstock.com:
19; MCarter/Shutterstock.com: 9; Nastenok/Shutterstock.com:
cover, 1; Phil McDonald/Shutterstock.com: 5; Vaclav Volrab/
Shutterstock.com: horseshoes; Zuzule/Shutterstock.com: 15

ISBN 9781626870024
LCCN 2013947281

Printed in the United States of America
Mankato, MN
November, 2013
PA02195

ABOUT THE AUTHOR

Pamela Dell is the author of more than fifty books for young people. She likes writing about four-legged animals as well as insects, birds, famous people, and interesting times in history. She has published both fiction and nonfiction books and has also created several interactive computer games for kids. Pamela divides her time between Los Angeles, where the weather is mostly warm and sunny all year, and Chicago, where she loves how wildly the seasons change every few months.

CONTENTS

Horses of the West

A horse comes racing across the Idaho plain. It is quick, strong, and sure-footed. It can climb rocky hillsides easily. Its coat has bright, bold spots. What is this powerful spotted horse? It is an Appaloosa.

This **breed** once carried Native Americans on buffalo hunts. But by the late 1800s, America's Appaloosas were almost all gone. Luckily, some lived on. Today, Appaloosas live in many parts of the world. Their special look makes them one of America's best-known breeds.

Sometimes you can feel an Appaloosa's spots! In winter, the spots sometimes have longer hair.

This Appaloosa lives on a farm.

What Do Appaloosas Look Like?

Appaloosas come in many colors, and they are best known for their spots. The spots are different sizes and shapes. They show up in different places, too. Some Appaloosas have spots all over. Others have only a few spots—or none at all.

People have given names to the patterns of spots. A big patch of white over the back and hips is a **blanket**. It looks like a blanket thrown over the horse.

> Some Appaloosas have plain white blankets. Others have blankets with spots.

Some Appaloosas have a *leopard* pattern. They are white with dark spots. *Snowflake* Appaloosas are just the opposite. They are dark with light spots. *Marble* Appaloosas are lightly colored with really tiny dark spots. *Frost* Appaloosas are dark with tiny light spots.

> Many Appaloosas have dark and light stripes on their hooves.

This Appaloosa has a blanket pattern.

Appaloosas have spots on their skin, too! In fact, they are known for their **mottled** skin. The skin is pink with dark dots. You can see it around their noses and mouths.

Appaloosas' eyes are different, too. Most horses have eyes that look all dark. On people's eyes, you can see white around the outside. You can see the white on an Appaloosa's eyes, too.

A horse's height is measured from its **withers** to the ground. Appaloosas measure about 57 to 61 inches (145 to 155 centimeters). They are not very heavy horses. Most of them weigh 950 to 1,175 pounds (430 to 530 kilograms).

People often use the word hands to say how tall a horse is. A hand is 4 inches (10 cm). Appaloosas are about 14 hands high.

This Appaloosa has a leopard pattern.

Newborn Appaloosas

Newborn Appaloosa **foals** have long, skinny legs. But they can stand up soon after they are born. The mother keeps a close watch on her foal. The foal drinks its mother's milk to grow strong. After a while, it starts eating other foods.

Appaloosa foals sometimes change color as they grow up. Lighter-colored foals often get darker when they lose their baby hair. Gray foals get lighter as they grow.

Appaloosa foals can look very different from their parents. And spots and colors sometimes change as the horses age.

This Appaloosa foal is enjoying a spring day.

This painting of spotted horses comes from the Pech Merle cave in France.

Appaloosas in History

Spotted horses have been around for thousands of years. People even drew pictures of them long ago. These **ancient** spotted horses were not Appaloosas. Europe and Asia had many types of horses. Some of them happened to have spots.

North and South America had no horses when Europeans arrived. Some of the Europeans' horses got loose. Native Americans quickly put them to use. Some Native groups made horses a big part of their lives.

Many people think Appaloosas came from Spanish **explorers'** horses. Some of these horses had spots—and some got loose. Native Americans traded the horses throughout the West. In the 1700s, Nez Percé Indians began raising them. They kept only horses that were fast, strong, brave, and smart. Not all of the Nez Percé's horses were spotted, but the spotted ones became the best known.

In ancient China, spotted horses were valued. An important book talked about "heavenly horses." People thought these might be spotted horses.

Soon, people knew a Nez Percé horse when they saw one. The Nez Percé lived in Idaho and Washington. They were near the Palouse (pah-LOOS) River. People called a Nez Percé horse "a Palouse horse." Over time, the words turned into "Appaloosa."

In 1877, the U.S. army drove the Nez Percé people from their homelands. Led by Chief Joseph, the Nez Percé headed for Canada. They rode over 1,300 miles (2,100 kilometers). Their fast, strong horses made them hard to catch. But the army caught them just outside Canada. The Nez Percé's horses were taken, given away, or left behind. The breed was almost lost.

Some people believe that Appaloosas came from Russian horses instead. They think Russian fur traders brought some spotted horses to America.

In the 1930s, some people became interested in Appaloosas again. They began to raise them. The Appaloosa Horse Club was started in 1938. This brought even more attention to the breed. Today, Appaloosas are well known and well loved.

Appaloosas need lots of space to run and rest.

What Are Appaloosas Like?

When strangers come near, Appaloosas sometimes get jumpy. But these horses like attention. If they feel safe, they are very friendly. And they are easy to handle.

Appaloosas are also smart and easy to train. Sometimes they can be stubborn. But most of them work very well with people.

These horses have lots of energy. They are strong and brave, too. And they are gentle and easygoing. They make good horses for young people or new riders.

Spending time with horses can help children with special needs. Gentle Appaloosas are good choices for this work.

These energetic Appaloosas are playing together.

Appaloosas at Work

In the late 1800s and early 1900s, people in the West loved circuses. Appaloosas often starred in Western circus shows. These horses had a smooth **gait**. They could stop, start, and turn quickly. They could do different tricks. People liked them for rodeos and roundup work, too.

Today, Appaloosas are known as all-around horses. They are still used for calf roping. They do well in horse shows, too. Some are trained for jumping. Appaloosas' strength and **endurance** make them great for cross-country races. And lots of people ride Appaloosas just for fun.

Endurance racers go 25 to 100 miles (40 to 161 km) in a single day! Some races are even longer. The horses might go 50 miles (80 km) each day.

This cowboy is riding an Appaloosa as he prepares to rope a steer.

Appaloosas Today

Years ago, Appaloosas were found only in North America. Now they are popular in other countries as well. There are Appaloosa horse clubs as far away as Australia. People raise Appaloosas in South America, too. The breed has become very popular in Europe.

People are working to keep Appaloosas from getting mixed with other breeds. This will help Appaloosas keep their special look. It will also help them keep their spirit.

Appaloosas do not live everywhere in the world yet. But people are finding out what wonderful horses they are. Someday, Appaloosas might be found in every country.

Some Appaloosas have a gait called the "Appaloosa ." This smooth, tireless gait is something like a running walk. The legs on the same side move together.

This young Appaloosa is enjoying a clear day. You can clearly see its leopard pattern.

Body Parts of a Horse

1. Ears
2. Forehead
3. Forelock
4. Eyes
5. Nostril
6. Muzzle
7. Lips
8. Chin
9. Cheek
10. Neck
11. Shoulder
12. Chest
13. Elbow
14. Forearm
15. Chestnut
16. Knee
17. Cannon
18. Pastern
19. Coronet
20. Hoof
21. Barrel
22. Fetlock
23. Hock
24. Tail
25. Gaskin
26. Stifle
27. Point of hip
28. Croup
29. Loin
30. Back
31. Withers
32. Mane
33. Poll

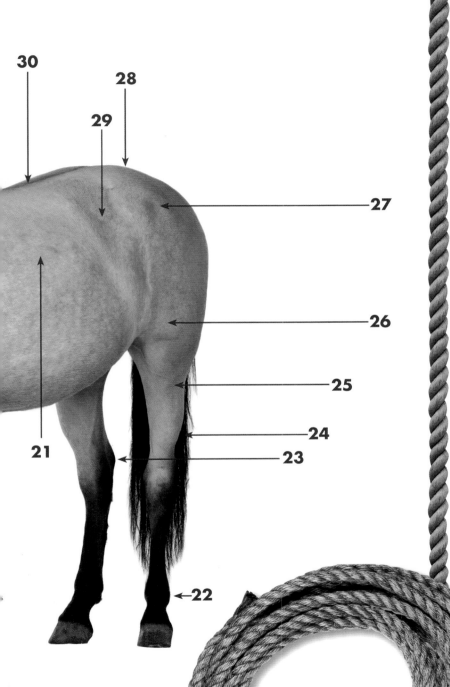

30
28
29
27
26
25
24
23
21
22

To Find Out More

IN THE LIBRARY

Gentle, Victor, and Janet Perry. *Appaloosas*. Milwaukee, WI: Gareth Stevens, 1998.

Patent, Dorothy Hinshaw, and William Muñoz (photographer). *Appaloosa Horses*. New York: Holiday House, 1988.

Sharp, Thelma, and Georgia Graham (illustrator). *The Saturday Appaloosa*. Calgary: Red Deer Press, 2001.

Stone, Lynn M. *Appaloosa Horses*. Vero Beach, FL: Rourke, 2008.

ON THE WEB

Visit our Web site for lots of links about Appaloosas:
www.childsworld.com/links

Note to Parents, Teachers, and Librarians: We routinely check our Web links to make sure they're safe, active sites—so encourage your readers to check them out!

Glossary

ancient (AYN-shunt) Something that is ancient is very old. Spotted horses are pictured in ancient art.

blanket (BLANK-et) A blanket is a type of pattern on an Appaloosa horse. It is a patch of white over the horse's back and hips.

breed (BREED) A breed is a certain type of an animal. Appaloosas are a colorful breed of horse.

endurance (en-DUR-untz) Endurance is being able to keep doing something that is very hard. Some Appaloosas take part in endurance races.

explorers (ex-PLOR-urz) Explorers travel to other places to see what they are like. Appaloosas might have come from Spanish explorers' horses.

foals (FOHLZ) Foals are baby horses. Appaloosa foals sometimes change color as they grow up.

gait (GAYT) A gait is a way of walking or stepping. Appaloosas are known for their smooth gait.

mottled (MOT-tuld) Something that is mottled has spots or patches of color. Appaloosas have mottled skin.

shuffle (SHUF-ul) A shuffle is a way of moving. You slide your feet along without lifting them high. Some Appaloosas have a special "Appaloosa shuffle."

withers (WIH-thurz) The withers is the highest part of a horse's back. An Appaloosa's height is measured at the withers.

Index